HELLO

MY NAME IS:

Oscar Richard Smith _ _ _ _ _

My birthday

04/06/2011

My signature

My
AWESOME
Year
Being

Published by Collins
An imprint of HarperCollins Publishers
Westerhill Road
Bishopbriggs
Glasgow G64 2QT

First edition 2020

10 9 8 7 6 5 4 3 2 1

ISBN 978-0-00-837264-4

A catalogue record for this book is available from the British Library

ACKNOWLEDGEMENTS
Publisher: Michelle I'Anson
Concept creator: Fiona McGlade
Author and Illustrator: Kia Marie Hunt
Project Manager: Robin Scrimgeour
Designer: Kevin Robbins
Photos © Shutterstock

Special thanks to the children at Golcar Junior Infant and Nursery School

Printed by GPS Group, Slovenia

MIX
Paper from
responsible sources
FSC
www.fsc.org **FSC™ C007454**

This book is produced from independently certified
FSC™ paper to ensure responsible forest management.

For more information visit: www.harpercollins.co.uk/green

My AWESOME Year Being

10

Written and illustrated by
Kia Marie Hunt

CONTENTS

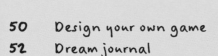

HELLO!

Your year being **10** is going to be **AWESOME**
now that you have this book to record it in!

You're about to discover **SO MANY** fun activities,
projects, recipes, and other exciting new
things to try...

Start by writing your name, birthday,
and signature just inside the front cover
— and draw something awesome!

Near the end of the book, there are blank pages
where you can continue with any of the activities,
try something again, or just do whatever you like!

Just inside the back cover, track your highlights
by writing one for each week of your awesome year
being 10!

P.S. You might need a grown-up's help to do some of the things
in this book, so ask them to read the note on page 128.

RULES

1. Fill in the pages **in any order** you like.

2. You could use **pencils, pens, crayons** or **paints** to answer the questions. You could also stick in photos or make a collage of different materials. Feel free to make a **mess**!

3. See any uncoloured drawings? Why not **colour them in**?

4. See any white spaces? Why not add your own **doodles**?

5. Complete the book how you want. There's no right or wrong way to express yourself!

6. **HAVE FUN** and remember that you are **awesome**!

ALL ABOUT ME

These pages are all about **YOU**, the awesome
10-year-old reading and completing this book!

Name: Oscar Smith

Height: 135cm

Hair colour: Brown

Eye colour: Blue

3 things I love to do:

1. Play video games

2. Climb

3. Golf

A fun fact about me:

If you were a character in a story, how would the author introduce you? Write a short **DESCRIPTION** of yourself in the third-person point of view...

. . . .

. . . .

. . . .

. . . .

. . . .

. . . .

. . . .

. . . .

Who got **THIS BOOK** for you?

(Remember to thank this person... if they got you this book, they're obviously pretty great!)

MY AWESOME LIFE

Where do you **LIVE**?

Draw your home, or stick in a photo.

TF29YQ

Who do you **LIVE WITH**?

Draw them here, or stick in photos.

Mom, Isla, Dad, Fergie, Shelbei

A DAY IN MY LIFE

What is it like to live a day in your awesome life? Write down your **DAILY ROUTINE**, including things like: what you do when you **WAKE UP** in the morning, what you **EAT**, what you do **AFTER SCHOOL**, and what you do **BEFORE BED**.

Time	Activity

9 THINGS I LIKED
ABOUT BEING 9

What were the 9 best things about being a 9-year-old?
Write or draw them on the posters.

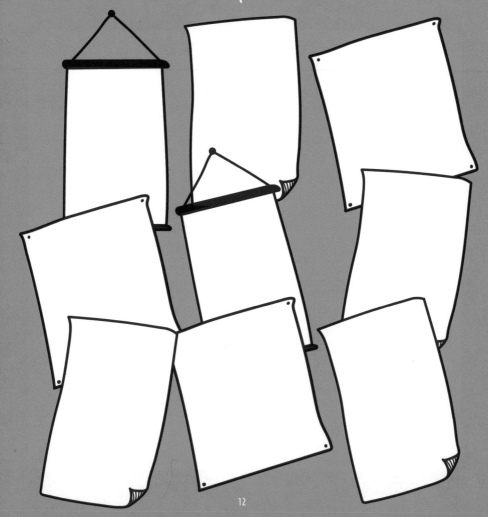

11 THINGS I'D LIKE TO DO BEFORE I'M 11

Think of 11 things you want to do
before you are 11 years old. They could
be anything from trying something
you've never done before, to visiting
somewhere new. Write a list and tick
each one off when you've done it!

You don't
have to do
all this in one
go. You can add
some things then
come back to
it later.

1 ....

2 ....

3 ....

4 ....

5 ....

6 ....

7 ....

8 ....

9 ....

10 ....

11 ....

MY SELF-PORTRAIT PHOTOSHOOT

You can draw instead if you prefer!

Get your camera ready, because you have 5 **SELF-PORTRAIT** photoshoot challenges to complete!

1. Stick in a photo of yourself smiling.

2. Stick in a photo of yourself pulling a silly face or with a funny filter.

SELFIE!

14

3. Stick in a photo of yourself in your favourite outfit.

4. Stick in a photo of yourself at your favourite place.

5. Stick in an action shot of yourself.

(You could be running, jumping in the air, dancing, or in the middle of another activity!)

MY MUSIC

What kind of **music** do you like to listen to?

....

....

What do you usually listen to music on?

My ALEXA

Who are your **top 5** favourite singers or bands?

① Weekend

② Aquilo

③ Oasis

④ Cyyo

⑤

What is your favourite **song**?

....

MY FAVOURITE LYRICS

When you listen to a song, do you mostly focus on the **sounds** of the music or the **words** (lyrics)?

Write down your **favourite line** from a song:

Why do you like these lyrics?

Do they remind you of anything? Like a person, a place or a feeling?

MY PLAYLIST

Make a **playlist** of all the best songs from your year as a 10-year-old. Every time you hear a **song** you really like, write it down here, along with **who sings it** and **why you like it**.

Some songs might be ones that have made you laugh, some might remind you of a place or a person, and some might just be songs you think are great!

1. Name of song: . . . .

    Who sings it: . . . .

    Why I like it: . . . .

2. Name of song: . . . .

    Who sings it: . . . .

    Why I like it: . . . .

3.   Name of song: . . . .

Who sings it: . . . .

Why I like it: . . . .

4.   Name of song: . . . .

Who sings it: . . . .

Why I like it: . . . .

5.   Name of song: . . . .

Who sings it: . . . .

Why I like it: . . . .

6.   Name of song: . . . .

Who sings it: . . . .

Why I like it: . . . .

SWIMMING OUTDOORS

Have you ever been swimming outdoors? You should try it! You could visit a **LAKE**, a **LIDO**, or even go swimming in the **SEA**.

BE SAFE!
Always go swimming outdoors with a grown-up.

Date:

WHERE did you go swimming?

Sea

Draw or stick in a photo of **YOURSELF SWIMMING**:

WHO did you go with?

What was your **FAVOURITE PART** of the experience?

What was your **LEAST FAVOURITE PART** of the experience?

It was super cold

Would you go swimming outdoors **AGAIN**? Why or why not?

Rate your experience:

MY ADVENTURES

Where I've BEEN:

(Write down the names of some interesting places you've visited on the postcards.)

Where I'd LIKE TO GO:

(Write down the names of some interesting places you'd like to visit in the future on the suitcases.)

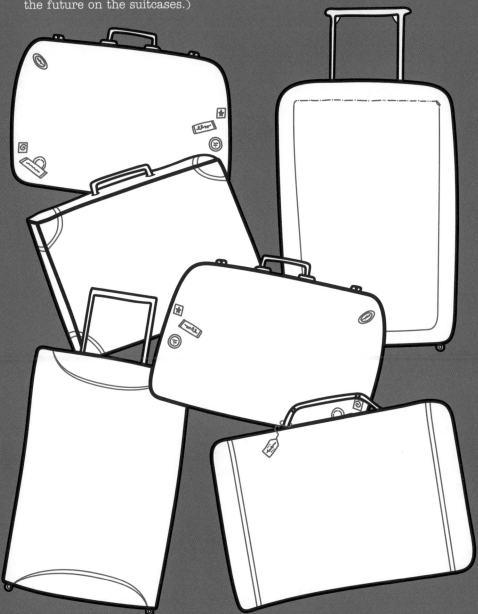

RECIPE: **MAKE YOUR OWN GNOCCHI**

BE SAFE! Get a grown-up to help.

Ingredients

- 3–5 baked potatoes (you can use leftovers if you like)
- 2 large eggs
- 150g of plain flour
- 2 tablespoons of grated cheese
- 1 teaspoon of nutmeg (optional)
- A pinch of salt and pepper
- A sauce of your choice (why not try pesto or tomato pomodoro?)

How to make

1. Cut the cooked potatoes in half and scoop the insides out of the skin and into a bowl. (The potato should be slightly warm, so if you're using leftovers ask a grown-up to help you reheat them just a little bit.)
2. Mash the potato with a fork, masher, or potato ricer to get rid of any lumps.
3. Separate the eggs and add the yolks into the bowl along with the cheese, salt, pepper, and nutmeg.
4. Mix it all together with your hands, adding the flour bit-by-bit until it feels like playdough.
5. Split the dough into 4 sections. On a flat surface sprinkled with some flour, roll each section of dough into a long thin sausage, then cut it into small pieces about 2.5cm long and 1.25cm thick.
6. Lightly roll a fork along each piece to give the gnocchi its pattern. (This will help your sauce stick to it!)
7. Ask a grown-up to help you add your gnocchi to a saucepan of boiling salted water. Only put in about 10 pieces at a time, they should float to the top when they are cooked (after about 30 seconds).
8. Serve your fresh gnocchi with a tasty sauce of your choice and a small sprinkling of cheese on top.

What did your finished meal **LOOK** like?

Draw it or stick in a photo.

What **SAUCE** did you serve your gnocchi with?

What was your **FAVOURITE THING** about making gnocchi?

Will you make it again?

Rate this recipe out of 10

1=Yuck!
10=Yum!

MY SCHOOL

What is your school called?

Priestlee Primary

What **year** are you in?

Year 6

Describe how you **feel** about school in 3 words:

Fun   Exiting   Weird

What is your **favourite subject**? Why?

Maths, because I love being pushed to the limits
and solving problems.

What is your **least favourite subject**? Why?

Geography don't know why but find it boring
but am quite good at it.

Have you ever had to **move**
from one school to another? _Never_____ _ _ _ _ _

What do you think is the most **difficult** thing about
moving from one school to another?

_Losing friends_____ _ _ _ _ _ _ _ _ _ _ _ _ _

_ _

What is the **best** thing about moving schools?

Making new friends and trying new things _

_ _

If you had to start at a new school with a **completely
new** and mysterious **identity** or disguise,
who would you be?

Write or draw your answer!

Mick

MY FRIENDS

Who are your FRIENDS?

List their names and write down where you met them, and what you like most about them.

Name of friend	Where I met them	What I like most about them

What do you **LIKE TO DO** with your friends?

Stick your **FAVOURITE PHOTO** of you and your friends
here (or draw if you prefer) and decorate the frame:

I ♡ MY FRIENDS

Write
more about
your **best
friend** on
page 56.

29

OPEN-AIR CINEMA

Take a trip to an open-air film screening, or you could set up your own **outdoor cinema** experience!

What you will need

- Something to watch a film on (this could be a tablet, laptop, or a projector and a white sheet).
- Somewhere to sit (you could sit on chairs or a blanket in the garden, or a tent if the weather is bad).
- And of course, some cinema snacks! (Why not make your own popcorn? See pages 76–79).

Date: ....

Where did you have your outdoor cinema experience?

....

Draw what it looked like or stick a photo here:

Rate this experience out of 10

⭐

1=Awful
10=Awesome

What film did you watch?

. . . .

Who did you watch it with?

. . . .

What cinema **snacks** did you eat?

. . . .

What was your **favourite part** of the experience?

. . . .

. . . .

. . . .

. . . .

Would you visit (or make) an outdoor cinema again?
Why or why not?

. . . .

. . . .

BEING A 10-YEAR-OLD VOLUNTEER

Your challenge is to spend some of your time **VOLUNTEERING** for a charity or cause you care about. You might be surprised at how much you enjoy it!

Here are some ideas:

- Love animals? Do some work at an animal shelter.
- Help out at a charity shop and donate your old toys and clothes there.
- Look after the environment by helping to clean up your community or volunteering at a nature reserve.
- Support other people that need your help by getting involved at a food bank or soup kitchen.

You could volunteer just once, for an hour or two, or you could volunteer every single week — it's up to you!

WHERE did you volunteer?

. . . .

WHY did you choose this charity or cause?

. . . .

. . . .

WHAT KIND OF THINGS did you have to do?

. . . .

. . . .

. . . .

What was your **FAVOURITE PART** of the experience?

. . . .

. . . .

. . . .

Did it feel **GOOD** to spend some of your time helping out?

. . . .

Would you volunteer again? Why or why not?

. . . .

. . . .

33

EARTH
IN 100 YEARS

Our planet is always changing. **Imagine** what life on Earth might be like in **100 years'** time.

Things to think about:

- Do you think people will look after the planet? Will Earth still be a good place to live in the future? Or will the climate be too different?
- What do you think will still be the same and what will change? Maybe there will be a new invention or technology that has changed everything!

100 YEARS FROM NOW...

Use this space to write about what you think life might be like, or how the world might look.

I think we will become more advanced in technolijy from finding power sources in space and we will stop using fossil fuels since they will be coming to shorts supply because they take millions of years to be made. If you have alot of mony then you can take a trip to space. I also think that another virus will come out and will be super dangerous.

MY FAVOURITE BOOK

Write down the **TITLE** and **AUTHOR** of your favourite book.

WHAT HAPPENS in the book?

WHY is this book your favourite?

How does reading this book make you **FEEL**?

If you could be a **CHARACTER** in the book, who would you be and why?

If you could **CHANGE ONE THING** in the book, what would it be?

Have you read any **OTHER BOOKS** by this author?

If yes, which ones? If no, why not try one? List any you like the sound of.

BEING A 10-YEAR-OLD BOOKWORM

Whenever you read a book, record the title and author here, rate it out of 10, and fill in a **book review**.

Title

Author

Rating

What did you think of the book?

1=Awful
10=Awesome

You can do more book reviews on the blank pages at the end of this book if you like!

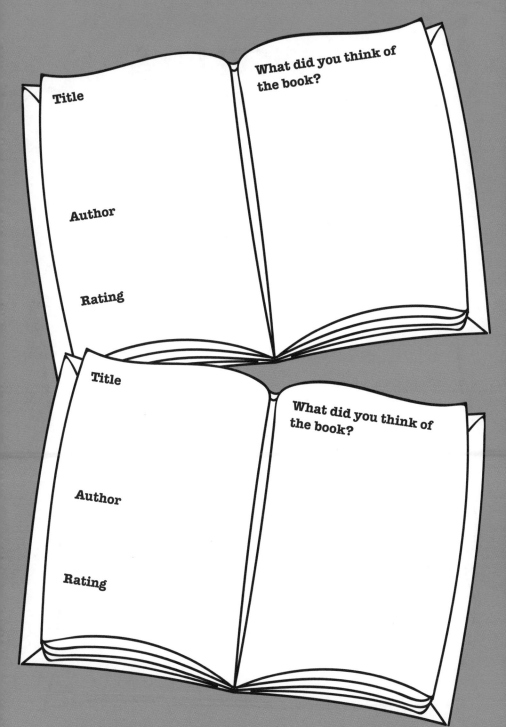

Title

Author

Rating

What did you think of
the book?

Title

Author

Rating

What did you think of
the book?

ENDANGERED & EXTINCT ANIMALS

Research an amazing animal that is
ENDANGERED and fill out the **FACT FILE** below.

Name of **animal**:

~~T-rex~~ Snow leapoard

What does it **look like**?

Draw it or stick in a picture.

Where does it **live**?

~~Australia~~ snowy climate

What makes it **amazing**?

Its bite force is extremely
strong and it is big cat with a thin coat

Why is it an **endangered** species?

I gets hunted

40

Research an amazing animal that has already gone **EXTINCT** and fill out the **FACT FILE** below.

Choose one that you wish was still around today!

Name of **animal**:

..... T-rex .....

What did it **look like**?

Draw it or stick in a picture.

Where did it **live**?

....

Why did it go **extinct**?

....

Why do you **wish** it was still around today?

....

....

VISITING A CAVE

Ask a grown-up to help you find a cave, and go with you!

Caves are truly unique and exciting places to visit!
Take a **trip to a cave** and record your experience here:

Date:

What cave did you visit? **Where** was it?

Describe the **atmosphere** inside the cave in **3 words**:

Write a **short story** about someone who finds
something special hidden inside a cave:

_____

_____

_____

_____

_____

_____

_____

_____

_____

_____

_____

_____

_____

_____

_____

_____

_____

_____

_____

_____

TWO TRUTHS AND A LIE

Here's a fun game to test how well people really know you! In any order you like, write down 3 THINGS about yourself. 2 of them should be TRUE and 1 of them should be a LIE that you made up.

① ....

....

② ....

....

③ ....

....

Show them to a friend or family member and ask them to guess which one is the lie. Who did you ask?

Which one did they think was the lie? _____

Were they right? _____

Now **ask the other person** to write down
2 TRUTHS and **1 LIE** about themselves and you
have to guess which is the lie!

1 ....

....

2 ....

....

3 ....

....

Which one do you think is the lie? _ _ _ _ _ _ _ _ _ _ _

Ask them to reveal the answer. Did you get it right?

_ _

Did you think it was easy or difficult to guess which one
was the lie?

_ _

_ _

MY FAVOURITE GAME

What is your favourite **GAME**?

....

What is the game **ABOUT**?

....

....

HOW do you play this game?

....

....

....

....

How **OFTEN** do you play it?

....

WHO do you like to play it with?

. . . .

WHERE do you like to play it?

. . . .

WHY is it your favourite game?

. . . .

. . . .

. . . .

DRAW something from your favourite game or stick in a photo.

GAME TRACKER

Every time you play a GAME THAT YOU LIKE, write down the name of it here, along with the reason why you like it.

This game tracker is for any kind of game, including board games, playground games, online games, imaginary games, video games, or apps!

Date	Game	Why I like it

Date	Game	Why I like it

DESIGN YOUR OWN GAME

You've written all about the games you like to play, now it is time to **design your own**!

Here are some ideas to inspire you:

- Grab some coloured paper and pens, and make your own board game that you can play with your family or friends.
- Make up a new game or sport for the Olympics, write down the rules and the names of the equipment that players will need.
- Create your own trading card game where players need to trade and collect all of the cards or characters for points.
- Draw or write about a completely new imaginary world, character, or storyline that could be part of a video game or app.
- There are lots of computer programs and phone apps out there that let you design and build your very own game. Ask a grown-up to help you download one of them, then get started!

What **kind** of game did you design, imagine or create?

What is it **called**?

Draw or stick a **photo** of your game, game designs, or game plans here:

What is the **aim** of the game? How do you **win**?

DREAM JOURNAL

Keep this book close to your bed along with a pen.

Whenever you have any strange or interesting DREAMS, write about them (or draw them) as soon as you wake up and see how many details you can REMEMBER!

Date:

Date:

53

PITCHING AN IDEA

Imagine you had to persuade an investor to buy your **product, invention,** or **business idea**.

What would your idea be?

(Draw it or write about it, and give it a cool name too!)

Who is your product, invention, or business idea for?

(Who would buy it or use it?)

. . . .

. . . .

. . . .

What is so special about your product or idea?

(How would you persuade the investor to give you money for it?)

. . . .

. . . .

. . . .

. . . .

Do you think you would be successful? Why or why not?

. . . .

. . . .

. . . .

MY IDEA

MY BEST FRIEND

Who is your best friend?

Fill out the **FACT FILE** below (you might need to interview your best friend to find out some of the answers).

Name: . . . .

. . . .

Birthday:

. . . .

What are their favourite **hobbies**?

. . . .

. . . .

What is their favourite **book**?

Draw your best friend or stick a photo here:

. . . .

. . . .

What is their favourite **song**?

....

What is their favourite **film**?

....

What is their favourite **food**?

....

Can you find out 3 interesting **facts** or secrets about them?

1. ....

2. ....

3. ....

What do you like **most** about your best friend?

....

What do they like most about **you**?

        ....

MY TEACHERS

Your teachers always give you a report about how you are doing at school, so now it's your turn to **WRITE THEIR REPORT**!

REPORT CARD

(A+)

Name of your teacher:

. . . .

What do you **like best** about them?

. . . .

What are they really **good at**?

. . . .

What advice would you give your teacher about how they could **improve**?

. . . .

. . . .

Who has been your **favourite** teacher so far and why?

. . . .

. . . .

What do you think makes a **good teacher**? Are there any skills or personality traits that a good teacher has to have?

. . . .

. . . .

. . . .

Do you think **you** would be a good teacher? Why or why not?

. . . .

. . . .

. . . .

. . . .

RISING WITH THE SUN!

Watching the **sun rise** is spectacular, and it's something that everyone should do at least once. You'll need to get up **early**, but it will be worth it!

The time that the sun rises changes depending on the day, the season, and your location, so make sure you plan ahead for your special sunrise experience:

Date that I will watch the sun rise:

Where I will be watching the sun rise:

Time that the sun will rise:

Time I will need to set my **alarm** for:

What I will need to do or take with me:

TIP

Take a camera with you to snap a photo of the sunrise!

Or make a time-lapse video (see page 62).

ON THE DAY

What is the **weather** like?

Tell a grown-up, or ask one to go with you.

Did you enjoy watching the sunrise? What did you **like** the most?

Draw the sunrise or stick a photo here:

FILMING A TIME-LAPSE

A **time-lapse** is a **video** that's usually quite short, but it shows a lot of time passing by.

A time-lapse video is made up of many **photos** in a row, each taken in the same place but at different times. They should be taken at different time intervals depending on what you'd like to capture, for example:

- If you'd like to film something that happens quite quickly, like traffic moving or people walking down a busy street, you should take a photo every few seconds.
- If you're filming something that happens a little slower, like a sunrise (pages 60–61) or the clouds moving, take a photo every few minutes.
- If you're filming something that happens very slowly, like a plant growing, you should take a photo every few days.

There are 2 secret **tips** you should follow to make sure you end up with a good time-lapse video.

1. Set up a stand or tripod for your camera, to make sure that each photo is taken from **exactly** the same place, position and angle.
2. When you have all your photos, you'll need to put them together (in order) to turn them into a time-lapse video. There are lots of apps you can do this with, or you can use websites that convert JPGs (still photos) to GIFs (moving photos) or MP4s (videos).

P.S. If you have access to a phone with a 'time-lapse mode' as one of the camera settings, you can use this as an easy-peasy way to film a time-lapse video without all the fuss!

Date: _____

What did you choose as the **subject** of your time-lapse video?

_____

How did you film it? And what with?

_____

_____

What was the **finished result** like? Is your time-lapse video **fun** to watch?

_____

_____

What was your **favourite part** of the process?

_____

What **other** things would you like to film as time-lapses?

_____

_____

_____

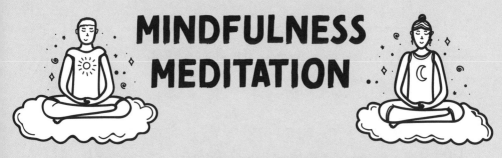

MINDFULNESS MEDITATION

We spend lots of our time thinking about the future, the past, and lots of other things, but we don't spend much time thinking about the present moment, **RIGHT NOW**.

Mindfulness helps us to become masters of our own minds. We can notice what we are thinking about and when, and we can use this power to enjoy being **COMPLETELY IN THE MOMENT**.

This meditation is a fun way to be mindful. It's called **'BALLOON BREATHING'**.

1. Sit down somewhere comfortable where you won't be disturbed.
2. Close your eyes and think about how you are breathing. Try to make your breaths slower and deeper.
3. As you breathe in, expand your belly like you are blowing up a big balloon.
4. As you breathe out, let the air out of the balloon slowly, through your nose.
5. Focus on how your body feels as you breathe in and out.
6. After some time, your thoughts might wander to something else. Once you realise your mind has wandered, take a moment to notice what you were thinking about. Then, try to move your focus back to thinking about your Balloon Breathing again.
7. See if you can focus on your Balloon Breathing for a few more minutes.

Date: _____

How did you feel **BEFORE** trying the Balloon
Breathing meditation?

_____

_____

Did your mind **WANDER OFF**? What kind of things did
you start to think about?

_____

_____

How did you feel **AFTER** finishing your meditation?

Would you try mindfulness meditation again?
Why or why not?

_____

_____

_____

_____

PUTTING THE 'FUN' IN FUNDRAISING!

It's challenge time! Your challenge here is to plan and organise a fundraiser for **CHARITY**. It can be something small or a big event, it's completely up to you!

There are only 2 **RULES**:

1. All money raised must go to a charity.
2. Have fun with it!

The **first** step is to decide which charity you are going to raise funds for.

WHICH charity would you like to raise money for?

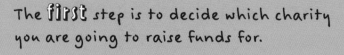

WHY have you chosen this charity?

The **second** step is to decide how you are going to raise money. Here are some fundraiser ideas:

Book sale

Cake sale

Auction
(or silent auction)

World record
attempt

Sponsored
run

Raffle

Clothes
swap

Beetle
drive

Charity
walk

Silent
disco

HOW will you raise money? What kind of fundraiser will you organise?

The **third** step is asking someone for help. Even the most amazing fundraiser needs a good team! You could ask your family, a friend, or even your teacher at school to help you bring your fundraising idea to life.

WHO will be on your fundraising team?

Now it is time to put your fundraising plan together. Here are some other questions to think about:

- Where and when will your fundraiser take place?
- What do you need to do to prepare?
- How much money do you want to raise?
- How will you collect the donations?
- How will you let people know about your fundraiser? You will need to make sure people know about it, so that they can come along!

DATE of fundraiser:

How much **MONEY** did you raise for your charity?

What was the most **DIFFICULT** thing about planning your fundraiser?

What was the **BEST** thing about planning your fundraiser?

Stick some photos from your fundraising experience here, or draw something:

Would you do it **AGAIN**? (Why or why not?)

MY FAVOURITE FILM

What is the name of your favourite **FILM**?

HOW MANY TIMES have you watched it? _____

When and where did you see it for the **FIRST TIME**?

What is the film about? Write a film **SYNOPSIS**
(a short description of what happens).

If you could be any **CHARACTER** in the film, which one would you be?

If you could make up a different **ENDING** to the film, what would happen? What would change and what would stay the same?

_____

_____

_____

_____

_____

_____

BEING A 10-YEAR-OLD
FILM CRITIC

Colour in the stars to give your rating.

Whenever you watch a new film, write down the name of it and fill in your own **FILM REVIEW**.

Name of film

Review

Rating ☆☆☆☆☆

Name of film

Review

Rating ☆☆☆☆☆

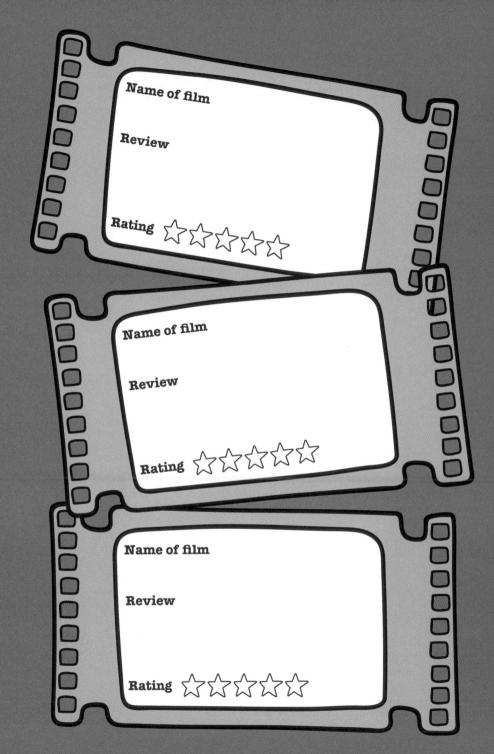

Name of film

Review

Rating ☆☆☆☆☆

Name of film

Review

Rating ☆☆☆☆☆

Name of film

Review

Rating ☆☆☆☆☆

VISITING A CASTLE

Whether they are just historic ruins left in the ground, or they are complete with impressive towering turrets, all **CASTLES** are fun to visit!

TAKE A TRIP to a castle (ask a grown-up to help you find a castle that you can travel to and visit) and record your experience here:

Date: ....

WHAT CASTLE did you visit?

....

....

WHERE was it?

....

....

WHO did you go with?

....

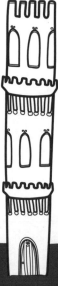

....

What did it **LOOK LIKE**?

Draw it
or stick in
a photo.

What were your **FAVOURITE THINGS** about the castle?

. . . .

. . . .

. . . .

. . . .

. . . .

. . . .

RECIPE: **PERFECT POPCORN (YOUR OWN WAY!)**

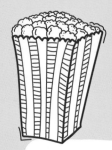

Popcorn is the perfect **snack**. Making it at home is easy, and it means that you can add whichever flavour you like!

What you'll need

- 50g of popping corn (kernels)
- A microwaveable bowl **OR** a pan (both with a lid)
- A little bit of oil (when making on the stove)

Ask a grown-up to help you, and make sure that you safely pop the corn without burning it!

BE SAFE!

You can pop the corn in 2 different ways:

In the microwave

1. Add the kernels to the bowl and put the lid on.
2. Put the bowl in the microwave on high for a few minutes; the popcorn will quickly begin to pop!
3. Once all of the amazing popping sounds start to slow down so that there are a couple of seconds between each pop, you should stop the microwave and carefully remove the bowl with oven gloves.

On the stove

1. Put a little bit of oil into the pan and wait for it to heat up.
2. Add the kernels to the pan and put the lid on; the popcorn will quickly begin to pop!
3. Once all of the amazing popping sounds start to slow down so that there are a couple of seconds between each pop, you should remove the pan from the heat.

Now you have your popcorn, it's time to add **flavour**! Here are some tasty recipes...

STICKY CARAMEL POPCORN CUPS

- Melt some butter in a pan.
- Gently stir in dark brown sugar until it dissolves into a yummy caramel syrup.
- Put your popcorn into cups and pour the sticky caramel over the top.
- Wait for it to cool down before you dig in!

PEANUT BUTTER POPCORN

- Add a bit of vegetable oil to a pan instead of butter.
- Then stir in honey, peanut butter, and a few drops of vanilla extract.
- Once it is runny, pour the peanut butter over the popcorn and wait about 5 minutes... then eat!

TOASTED COCONUT POPCORN

- For this recipe, simply cook your popcorn in coconut oil instead of butter or vegetable oil.
- Then, when it is all popped, mix in some toasted coconut flakes for a tropical twist!

GARLIC AND BASIL POPCORN

- Popcorn doesn't always have to be sweet!
- Try mixing your popped corn with a handful of chopped fresh basil leaves, some garlic salt, and a drizzle of olive oil for a salty, savoury treat.

BIRTHDAY CAKE POPCORN

- Add rainbow sprinkles and a drizzle of melted white chocolate to your popped corn!

Record your experience on the next page...

Date: ....

What kind of popcorn did you make?

....

Who did you make it with?

....

What did your popcorn look like?

Draw it or stick in a photo.

Rate this recipe out of 10

1=Yuck!
10=Yum!

What was your favourite thing about making popcorn?

....

....

Why not make up **your own flavour** combination?

Date: ....

What is the **name** of your popcorn recipe?

....

Write down the **ingredients** you used, and **how you made it**.

Ingredients	How to make
•	1. ....
•	2. ....
•	3. ....
•	4. ....
•	5. ....
•	6. ....

What did your popcorn **taste like?**

....

....

Rate this recipe out of 10

1=Yuck!
10=Yum!

MY PETS

Do you have any **PETS**?

If **YES**, choose one and fill out the pet fact file below!

If **NO**, fill out the fact file below for the pet you would love to have!

Name: ....

Type of animal: ....

What does it **look like**?

Draw it
or stick in
a photo.

What is SPECIAL about your pet?

What do you think is (or would be) the BEST THING about having a pet?

Imagine if you could TALK TO YOUR PETS (or other animals) and they could talk back.

WHICH ANIMAL would you talk to?

What would you ASK THEM?

What do you think they would SAY TO YOU?

MAKING A MINI JOURNAL!

The only thing more fun than using a mini journal or book for writing or drawing, is making the journal itself!

What you'll need

- A4 card for journal cover – the colour or pattern of your choice!
- B5 paper for journal pages, or A4 paper that you can trim
- 2 needles, one slightly larger than the other
- Some thread (waxed thread is best but any thread will do)
- Scissors
- A ruler
- Paperclips
- Some plain paper for making a template
- Decorations for your journal (photos, glitter, beads, stickers, tape – anything you like!)

BE SAFE!
Ask a grown-up for help when using a needle and thread.

How to make

1. First, carefully fold your A4 piece of card in half. This will be your **journal cover**.

2. Next, if you are using A4 paper, use a ruler and scissors to measure and trim 6 pages down to B5 size (25cm x 17.6cm).

3. Once you have 6 sheets of B5 paper, simply fold each one in half. These will be your **journal pages**.

4. Now, trim your plain sheet of paper down to B5 size and fold that in half too. This will be your **page template**.

5. Use your ruler to measure the height of your page template. Use the larger needle to poke a hole through the fold line, exactly in the centre.

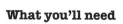

1st hole

6. Then poke a 2nd hole halfway between the centre hole and the top of the page, and a 3rd hole halfway between the centre hole and the bottom of the page.

7. Use the page template to poke 3 holes in exactly the same places on each of your journal pages and your journal cover too by lining the template up with each page, making sure the fold lines are in the same place, securing it with paper clips, then poking through the 3 template holes into the paper or card.

8. Now, place your journal cover (open) down on the surface and place all the pages on top of each other so that all the holes line up.

9. Thread the slightly smaller needle and pass it through the middle hole, pulling the thread through all the pages and out the other side of the journal cover.

10. Then, bring the needle and thread back in through the top hole, back out through the middle hole, and back in again through the bottom hole, like you're making a figure of 8 with your thread.

11. Once your thread has been through all 3 holes and gets back to the centre, tie it in a double knot or a bow with the tail of the thread to secure it and trim the ends off.

CONGRATULATIONS, you have just made your very own journal! Now you can **DECORATE** the cover and the pages however you like!

Turn the page...

Date: _____

What was your **FAVOURITE THING** about making your own journal?

_____

_____

What **COLOURS**, **PATTERNS**, or **DECORATIONS** did you use to make your journal **UNIQUE**?

_____

_____

Draw what your journal **LOOKS LIKE**, or stick in a photo:

What will you USE this journal for?

(It could be a diary, a photo album, a doodle book, a gift for someone, or a place to collect tiny things!)

doodle diary

_____

_____

_____

_____

_____

Will you make ANOTHER journal? Why or why not?

(You could experiment by making more pages, different sizes, or using different materials!)

_____

_____

_____

_____

_____

MY FAVOURITE SPORTS

What are your **top 3** favourite sports, exercises, or fitness activities?

1 ....

2 ....

3 ....

Write about **how often** you do each of your favourite sports or fitness activities, **where** you like to do them, and **who** you usually do them with:

....

....

....

....

....

....

....

....

....

....

Why do you like these sports or fitness activities so much?

....

....

....

....

....

How do they make you **feel**?

What is your proudest sports and fitness achievement or memory?

Describe it, draw it, or stick in photos.

MY TEAM

Write down the name of your favourite **SPORTS TEAM**.

(This could be any kind of team, whether it's a famous sports team that you support or a team that you play for as part of a sports club.)

WHAT KIND of sport does this team play?

WHY are they your favourite team?

Draw your favourite team's **LOGO**.
If they don't have one, make one up!

Draw it or stick in a photo.

GOING FISHING & CRAB LINING

Have you ever been **fishing** or **crab lining** (fishing for crabs) before? It's time to plan a trip!

Whether you have experienced it before or this is your first time ever, you're going to have a lot of fun! Here are some questions to help you plan...

Who will you go with?

Always ask a grown-up to help you with planning your trip and using equipment. Don't go fishing or crab lining alone!

Where will you go?

- If you're going **fishing** you'll need to choose whether you'll be sitting next to the water or sailing on the water.
- If you're going **crab lining**, you'll need a good place to sit and dangle your crab line down into the sea, such as a harbour.

What will you need?

Don't forget a fishing rod or crab line, bait (this will change depending on what you want to catch), and other things like drinks, snacks, warm clothes, suntan lotion, waterproofs and something to sit on.

ON THE DAY

Date: _____

What was the **weather** like? Colour in one or more.

Did you go **fishing** ☐ or **crab lining** ☐ ?

_____

How long did you spend doing this?

_____

What did you **catch**?

Write a list, draw your favourite catch, or stick in some photos.

What was your **favourite thing** about the day?

_____

_____

SCHOOL TRIPS

Think of your favourite school trip ever. It could be an **OVERNIGHT STAY** or just a class **DAY TRIP**!

WHERE did you go?

HOW did you get there?

WHAT did you do?

WHO did you spend the most time with?

What was the **FUNNIEST THING** that happened on the trip?

What was your **FAVOURITE PART** of the trip?

If you could plan your **DREAM SCHOOL TRIP**, where would you go? What would you do?

INVENTING MY OWN SECRET CODE

If you've ever wished you could communicate in your own **SECRET LANGUAGE**, now's your chance.

Use the table below to draw a **SYMBOL** for each of the letters of the alphabet.

For example, the letter A could be a swirl, the letter B could be a star, and so on. You can use the doodles around this page as inspiration for your symbols.

A	B	C	D	E	F	G	H	I

J	K	L	M	N	O	P	Q	R

S	T	U	V	W	X	Y	Z	.

Give your new secret code an awesome name:

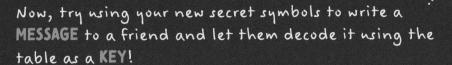

Now, try using your new secret symbols to write a **MESSAGE** to a friend and let them decode it using the table as a **KEY**!

Date:

WHO did you share your secret code with?

Did they correctly **DECODE** your message?

Rate this activity:

MY LIFE ONLINE

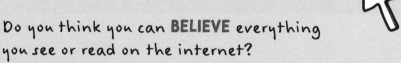

Do you think you can **BELIEVE** everything you see or read on the internet?

Write about something you've seen online that probably isn't as true or as real as it seems.

Lots of people think that the internet is the **GREATEST INVENTION** of all time.

Do you agree? Why or why not?

What do you think life was like **BEFORE** the internet existed?

How do you think having no access to the internet affects daily life?

_____

_____

_____

_____

_____

Show your answer to someone **OLDER** than you, who can remember a time before the internet existed (like a parent or grandparent).

Ask them what they think of your answer. What did they say? Did they laugh? Were you right or wrong?

_____

_____

_____

_____

_____

ON HOLIDAY

Think of a **holiday** or special **trip** you have been on in the past year. **Where** did you go?

(Describe where you went, draw a picture, or stick in a photo or map.)

Who did you go with?

. . . .

What did you **take** with you?

. . . .

. . . .

What did you **do**?

....

....

....

....

What was your **favourite part** of the holiday or trip?

....

....

....

....

If you could plan your **dream** holiday or trip,
where would you go and what would you do?

....

....

....

....

SHOPPING AND COOKING FOR THE FAMILY

On these pages you'll COOK a meal for your family. You'll also PLAN it all and SHOP for the ingredients — you're about to be one seriously impressive 10-year-old!

Date: _____

First things first, what MEAL will you cook?

_____

_____

HOW MANY people are you going to cook for? _____

What INGREDIENTS will you need?

(Use one colour to write the ingredients you already have available in the house, and another to write those you will need to buy from a shop.)

WHERE will you go to buy the ingredients?

HOW MUCH did your shopping cost? _____

Now you have all your ingredients ready, **HOW** will you make the meal? Write a step-by-step recipe guide:

BE SAFE!
Always ask a grown-up for help when using cooking equipment like knives, hot stoves, or ovens!

Did cooking your recipe go to **PLAN**?

What did your meal **LOOK LIKE**?

Draw it or stick in a photo.

WHO did you cook for?

Ask a member of your family to **RATE** the meal and write a short **REVIEW**.

Rate this meal out of 10

1=Yuck!
10=Yum!

What was the most **DIFFICULT** part of shopping and cooking for the family?

_____

_____

_____

Was it **EASY** to find the ingredients and pay for them?

(Is this something you do often? Or does someone else usually do those things?)

_____

What was the **BEST** thing about shopping and cooking for the family?

_____

_____

Will you shop and cook for the family again? Why or why not?

_____

_____

_____

MY STYLE

Describe your fashion **'style'** in 3 words:

1 _____

2 _____

3 _____

What is your favourite **outfit**?

Draw it or stick in a photo.

Where do you get your clothes from?

_____

_____

Design your **dream** outfit, costume, pair of shoes, or accessory:

Draw it or stick in a photo.

BEING A 10-YEAR-OLD CARTOGRAPHER

A **cartographer** is a person who draws or makes **maps**. Use the page opposite to design your own map.

It can be a map of somewhere you know (like your bedroom, house, or neighbourhood) or it can be a map of an imaginary place!

Date: _ _ _ _ _ _ _ _ _ _ _ _

Which **place** will you be designing your map for?

_ _ _ _ _ _ _ _ _ _ _ _ _ _ _ _

_ _ _ _ _ _ _ _ _ _ _ _ _ _ _ _

Use the table on the right to make your map **key**. This gives information needed to understand the map — you can use colours or symbols to explain where things are on the map.

Symbol or colour	Meaning
⌂	House
✗	Treasure!

Draw your awesome map.

Rate this activity:

VISITING A THEME PARK

Whether you're a big **THRILL SEEKER** or not, theme parks are always a fun day out with friends or family. Ask a grown-up to help you find a **THEME PARK** that you can travel to and visit. Record your experience here...

Date:

WHICH theme park did you visit?

WHO did you go with?

Which **RIDES** or attractions did you go on?

What was your **FAVOURITE THING** about your visit?

If you could **INVENT** a new theme park ride or attraction, what would it be?

Write about or draw it here.

BEING A 10-YEAR-OLD POTTER

A potter is a person who makes **pottery**.
Are you ready to become a potter for the day?

All you need is some **clay** – there are different options:

- You could buy some 'bake at home' clay from a shop and make something from it by following the packet instructions.
- You could order a DIY pottery or craft kit online.
- Or maybe you could ask a grown-up to help you book a visit to a pottery studio so you can have a go on a real potter's wheel.

Record your pottery experience here:

Date:

Where did you try pottery?

What did you **make**?

(It could be anything: a pot, a bowl, a vase, a plate, an animal, a jewellery holder, a tree, a decoration...)

Was it **easy** or **difficult** to make?

What did it **look like**?

Draw it or stick in a photo.

What was your **favourite part** of the experience?

PLANNING A TOUR

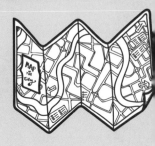

Visiting a new **TOWN** or **CITY** is always very exciting, but have you ever planned a **TOUR** yourself? Now's your chance!

How to do it

1. Work with a grown-up to help you choose where you could visit. It could be a faraway city, or simply a nearby town. They can help you with booking any travel or accommodation you need.

2. Use maps, books, and the internet (blog posts or travel vlogs can be very useful) to find out what there is to do and see there.

3. Write down any landmarks, sights, or attractions you would like to visit while you are there.

4. Work out how much time you will need at each place, how far apart they are from each other, and how much time you will need to get from one to the other.

5. Write out your plan for the day, including breaks for food and rest.

6. Show your town or city tour plan to a grown-up to see what they think. They will probably have some good tips to make your plan even better, and they can help find out if you will need to book any tickets or extra methods of transport.

7. Fill in your final plan on the opposite page.

8. Don't forget to make a list of things you will need to take with you.

WHICH city or town will you visit?

Now you are ready to set off on your tour adventure!

YOUR PLAN

YOU ARE HERE

Time	Place	Activity

Date of tour:

WHO did you go with?

HOW did you get there?

How easy or difficult was it to plan out your tour?

Did it go according to **PLAN**? If not, what happened?

What were the **3 BEST THINGS** about your tour experience?

1

2

3

SELF-CONFIDENCE

What does **confidence** mean to you?

_____

_____

Do you think you are a **confident person**?
Why or why not?

_____

_____

Can you remember a time when you did something
that you **needed extra confidence** for?

_____

_____

_____

How did doing that make you **feel**?

😏 😮 🙂 🤩 😎

Of all the people in your life, **who** makes you feel the most confident? (And how do they do that?)

Write about a confident person who you **admire**...

How are you **similar** to this person and how are you **different**?

Is there anything you can **learn** from this person about how to have more confidence in yourself?

DEAR FUTURE SELF...

Write a **LETTER** to your future self, 10 years from now, when you will be 20 years old.

Tell your future self about your life **NOW**, reminding them what it's like to be 10.

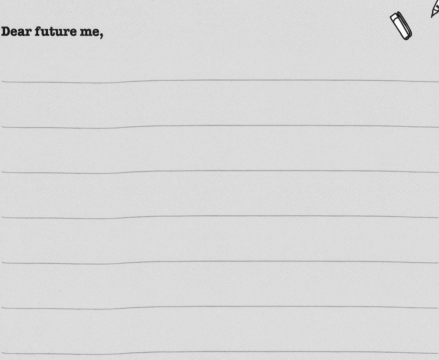

- Write down what your goals and ambitions are, so you can see if you achieved them.
- What do you hope will stay the same?
- What do you hope will have changed?

Dear future me,

_____

_____

_____

_____

_____

_____

_____

_____

_____

_____

_____

_____

_____

_____

_____

_____

_____

_____

_____

_____

(Remember to keep this book somewhere safe so that
you can read your letter in the future, and you can
always remember your awesome year being 10!)

MY AWESOME YEAR BEING **10**

You can write, draw, or stick things in!

121

124

A NOTE TO GROWN-UPS

You can join in the fun too by sharing experiences together, discussing the activities and celebrating accomplishments throughout the year! And remember to help with some of the recipes and other tricky tasks.

Follow us on Instagram @Collins4Parents where we'll be hosting regular competitions and giveaways as well as giving you extra ideas to make the year **even more awesome!** Share your experiences with the book using the hashtag #MyAwesomeYearBeing

MY AWESOME YEAR SERIES

9780008372606

9780008372613

9780008372620

9780008372637

9780008372644

MY YEAR IN HIGHLIGHTS

Each week, write **ONE SENTENCE** that describes your highlight of the past 7 days. It could be a funny moment, a special day out, or something else.

52 weeks in a year = 52 awesome highlights!

1
2
3
4
5
6
7
8
9
10
11
12
13
14
15
16
17
18
19
20
21